Refusing to Grow

The company that refused $1,000,000 profit,
because they couldn't ask a question.

By A. Ruben

Printed in the United States of America.

Refusing to Grow: the company that refused $1,000,000 profit, because they couldn't ask a question / Ruben

ISBN: 978-0-9754590-2-7

Ickynicks Publishing

Front Cover by Adam Zillins

The following story is based upon actual events and people. However the timeline of events has been compressed and edited to accommodate the story and its characters. Any similarity of dramatized characters, incidents, companies, or attributes to any actual person, living or dead, or to any actual event or to any existing organization is entirely coincidental and unintentional.

Note to the Reader

The following chronological series of semi-disconnected incidents are based on true events and characters, which capture certain personalities perhaps too ridiculous to imagine. Yet, they are neither exaggerations nor embellishments.

Preface

Long before Arthur became a teacher he had to pay his dues first. With the economic situation in the nation worsening, his prospects of teaching faded, as did his hope, but he still believed in his dream; in wake of tighter budgets, he competed however with thousands of other candidates, often for just one position. Unable to secure a teaching position and with student loans looming overhead he sought employment in sales.

He began in Los Angeles and later came to Cleveland, where this book begins. A hard worker, his efforts soon garnered the respect of his co-workers and those in management. Even his competition would soon respect him as a worthy adversary in the business arena. And yet, his success drew the envy of others. In LA, he clashed with the company's son, and in Cleveland he would discover a similar clash with the vice president of sales.

Arthur was successful in whatever he put his mind to, but for that he was envied. Whether in LA or in Cleveland, he went above and beyond, helping others, and increasing numbers, but always he held onto his dream. One day, he hoped, he might become a teacher; when the president in Cleveland referred to him as "vice president material" he felt proud of his accomplishments, but unfortunately that only exacerbated the clashes.

He was clever, thinking outside the box, finding ways to increase profits while still being careful in his approaches; he objectified his strategies, always keeping two feet on the ground and never pursuing lofty goals. Perhaps it was that he, like so many others, had stood in the unemployment line and Arthur made it his personal mission to do everything in his power to grow the company he was working for. He slashed costs, increased profits, sold at high margins and even exceeded his quota by double; never again did he ever want to stand in that line.

He believed in a strong set of morals and held himself to high standards. He advocated mutual respect and camaraderie and carried these with him wherever he went and worked; in LA he served as an executive and in Cleveland he was hired as its sales manager. When told he had to restructure, namely fire several employees, he instead cross-trained them and delivered overwhelming profit results.

In Cleveland, he doubled his quota while cleaning up a hornet's nest. Despite having earned the company over $630,000 in profit in less than a year he would be fired. His success had once again revealed that although others may ask for diligence and hard work they may feel threatened if that success towers over them; no amount of explanation could save Arthur. Neither the president nor the vice president of sales would listen; while one sold cheap the other slept with prostitutes.

Although Arthur finally did fulfill his dream what he had learned though was immeasurable. Perhaps it was naivety, but he truly believed that those employed were doing everything in their power to help those unemployed. Sadly, he discovered that was false. Instead, there was a colossal lack of accountability and counterintuitive policies.

While city and state budgets were hit, schools lost their funding, and workers were being told to make do with less the leadership was failing. Too many were just narrow-minded or simply fools, costing their companies growth and further setting the nation back; call it patriotism or pride, but Arthur believed that being an American meant being the best at what one did, whether as a worker, a manager, or a CEO. He felt it was about everyone helping each other, challenging one another, and those leading to set the example by shouldering the weight and leading the charge forward, headlong into whatever obstacle America faced. But perhaps that was just youthful foolishness.

Cast of Characters:

Arthur – A young sales manager who once aspired to be a teacher. After having stood in an unemployment line, he will strive to help others through sales. Leveraging his market, he will meet his quota by double.

Bruce – A president in his late fifties, his salesmanship philosophy will be based on 10% profit margin only, as he favors quantity over quality. He will insist that his sales team play to their market, not leverage it.

Ted – Vice-President, and also in his late fifties, his utter lack of censorship and overt sexism will discredit him in front of clients and employees alike. Refusing to accept any blame for his mistakes, he will instead point the finger at others. And after feeling threatened by Arthur's successes, he will terminate him.

Sheryl – The Director of Operations, her disorganization and refusal to accept accountability for her mistakes will further exacerbate the company's financial situation, eventually leading to its implosion.

Jimmy – the superintendent of the company as well as "Mr. Funny," his retirement will be indefinitely postponed as the dominos begin to tumble. He will appreciate Arthur's candor and efforts, and will regret his dismissal.

Florence – The Finance Manager, she will be blamed for Sheryl's erroneous reports as well as the company's impairing situation. As a result of her department spending more and more of its time trying to acquit itself of blame, implosion will become inevitable.

Acknowledgements

The author wishes to thank the following for their support, Lynn, Marilyn, Alex, Sara, Rochelle and Mike. Thank you very much for your assistance in making this work possible.

The following is based on a true story.

Chapters

The Sales Meeting

I.   The Interview

Arthur was being interviewed for a sales manager role. "I just want to tell you that we fired your predecessor twenty-four hours ago," said Ted, the Vice President. His tone was as serious as it was unforgiving. Wearing a turtleneck, he sat beside Bruce, the President, who was anything but smiling. In fact, the two men were seated across from him as though it were an interrogation. Both were studying him from head to toe, neither willing to offer a friendly invitation; although they had reached out to him, they remained reserved.

At almost thirty years old, Arthur certainly had the sales experience. Moreover, he had recently served on an executive team, having tripled his former company from two million dollars to ten, and having done so in a recession. As a result, he had caught the attention of numerous CEOs, including some Fortune 500 companies. Many had called him personally, offering him both high-ranking positions as well as incredible perks; one even offered to sell him half his business.

But despite the attention, Arthur remained humble. He had paid his dues, studying long hours in college, working three jobs to pay for his student loans and even toiling under the hot sun to earn his dollar. Moreover, he had learned humility, standing in long lines at the unemployment office when his teaching career was cut short by the recession. With only retail sales experience under his belt, he took a sales position and carved out a new path for himself.

In LA, he had proven himself an adept salesman as well as an executive, growing the business there in addition to negotiating with clients, venders and the unions; like a mineral vein unearthed, he discovered something about himself each time, tapping potential he never even knew he had. He proved to be imaginative, adaptive, and persistent; one CEO even remarked once how he achieved in six months what his most senior employee did in ten years.

Now as Arthur sat across from Bruce and Ted, he wondered what new challenges faced him.

"We're hoping you can do better," Ted said, faintly smiling. It was the first sign of any welcome.

"Well, I don't intend to disappoint," he replied.

"Then welcome aboard," Ted said, offering his hand. "And if you're as good as you say you are, then I can promise you one thing: this will be the last place you ever work."

II.   Regurgitation

It was 7:30 AM and as the sales meeting began Arthur was taken aback. More of a regurgitated exercise than a sales meeting he noticed that sales agents went around the table in a round robin, each one taking his or her turn to update Bruce on their progress. As each one spoke, the president entered the data into his laptop, which projected on a large screen against the wall; while one spoke the others sat quietly. It reminded him of grade school, particularly of how he had been instructed to rehearse what he had learned onto an exam; it was neither a teaching style he enjoyed nor wished to teach as a teacher.

Moreover, what learning actually took place? He could scarcely recall anything he had learned in high school; he had gone through the motions of school, but retained almost nothing of value; of four years of Spanish and he had only remembered what *bueno* meant, good. In a similar fashion to rehearsing, each sales agent updated Bruce with wins, losses, or follow-ups. And yet, the information was neither probed any further than one-

4

word responses; he neither asked why the agent lost the deal or won it. Instead, Bruce just recorded it. Even when the agent said he or she followed-up, he never asked how. He just typed.

Arthur was shocked to say the least, but the meeting was only just beginning. In addition to the rehearsals, the new data neither correlated to the week's prior data nor portrayed agent's quotas accurately or even reflected profit margins correctly. In regards to the first point, the data was almost totally useless since it failed to connect with earlier information: Bruce's spreadsheet was more like a list of recorded data than a measuring device. Although he did separate information into groups, it neither told him what was a prospective lead nor where the company should be focusing its time and resources.

"Remember, we bid everything," he said to the team, reminding them that everyone was a prospective customer; the value of filtering leads was apparently lost on him.

In regards to the second point, agents neither knew where they stood on their quotas nor were even sure Bruce often knew. In one instance, a saleswoman had earned the company about

$450,000. Unfortunately, since quotas were measured in terms of profit, not revenue, she had no idea where she stood; unless agents kept track themselves, they were at the mercy of the company disorganization.

Finally, Bruce always put 10% in the profit margin column that lined every entry. So, regardless of whether the agent sold higher or negotiated for lower, he or she received 10%. Again, this posed a major problem in assessing an agent's quota, since quotas were based on both estimated profits as well as final profits after the project was completed.

Arthur was astonished, but then all of a sudden everyone clapped. Obligatory applause.

"Good job," Bruce said, congratulating an agent for booking a sale. Apparently, any sale over ten thousand dollars merited a clap, anything less and everyone snapped a finger; it was the most apathetic applause Arthur had ever seen.

Less than spirited, the entire room was anything but enthusiastic to either clap or snap; everyone's face reminded Arthur of a kid getting an awful toy for his or her birthday. The mandatory recognition was there, but not the excitement. In fact, most if not all sighed quietly. Arthur could only wonder why. After all, the project was worth half a million dollars. Why would anybody lament over that?

"It's not the dollar value," a project manager said to him after the meeting. "It's the profit margin." As the man explained, the deal had been sold at less than 10% profit margin. "Now I have no room for mistakes," he said, blaming the president. "But what really gets me is that he approved the sale."

III.   <u>The Engineer</u>

During the meeting, someone's phone abruptly rang. When the agent went to answer it, Bruce shot him a look of disapproval. As Arthur soon learned, taking client's calls during the sales meeting was forbidden. More than once, Bruce had fired an agent for doing so.

* * * * * * * *

Bruce was an engineer. Everything he did was linear. There was neither any deviation nor elasticity; coloring outside the lines was strictly prohibited. To him, salesmanship was just another equation.

"Buddy look, it's real simple," he said to Arthur, patronizing him. "You take your cost, you add 10% for profit and then you sell the job. That's it! It's not that hard. It's just selling." To him, there was no secret to selling, no art or skill, just a simple cut, clear and dry process that bordered on robotic.

To Bruce, selling was as followed:

1. Bid Low.

2. Win the work.

3. Build relationships.

4. Repeat.

He bid low and insisted his sales agents do the same. He frequently reprimanded agents who tried to sell higher than 10% margin, alleging it was a waste of time. "You got to play to this market, and I know this market," he would say. "So, I'm telling you now, buddy boy. Don't go above 10%."

Unfortunately, it was this rigidity and narrow-minded approach that demoralized his agents, and perhaps explained why few if any showed any enthusiasm to selling. After all, if the company offered a bonus beyond the quota, why wouldn't an agent try to sell higher? "How many times do I have to tell you," he would say. "Sell at 10% and not a penny more!"

In one instance, another saleswoman wanted to push a new product into the market. Yet, despite being aware of the inherent risk of unforeseen problems, Bruce limited her to 10%.

Not surprisingly, there were problems, and as a result of the company trying to resolve them it lost whatever profit it hoped to make; moreover, she was blamed for the losses.

"You have to know your costs!" Bruce said, often reprimanding others for his own inelasticity. Yet even more depilating to sales agents however was the fact that the company losses were held against quotas. In one instance, an agent lost a $72,000 deal after it fell through; instead of just not counting it, the $7,200 of potential profit went against her quota, and subsequently put her further back from achieving any bonus for the year.

Moreover, Bruce's prohibition of answering calls during the sales meeting ran the risk of losing sales opportunities; by the time Arthur came onboard the story was legend: an agent had once been expecting a call, but unable to take it because of Bruce she had to decline it, only to later discover her client had given away the contract to the competition. The deal had been worth $180,000. Consequently, she was fired.

As was always the case in failure, Bruce blamed the agent. "I hired you do a job right," he frequently said. As Arthur was to learn, his inflexibility and refusal to accept accountability led not just to repeated company losses but also company-wide disenchantment. Moreover, his rigidity further plagued the sales meetings because of how long it ran. Usually lasting between 2-3 hours, it often meant agents fidgeted the entire time, declining on average half a dozen calls. As a result, agents sped through the meeting as fast as possible: updates on wins and losses were kept brief, almost always one-word responses, and nobody elaborated on follow-ups.

"I left a voicemail yesterday," said one. "I sent an email," said another, and apparently that was good enough for Bruce.

IV.   Inflexibility

Even the clap or snap was kept short. The sales meeting was one of the most important ways that Bruce projected ahead, and his agents did everything they could to rush through it.

* * * * * * * * *

In addition to his stringent policies, which too often resulted in lost deals or ruined client relationships, it also cost the company valuable manufacturers. In the instance of the saleswoman mentioned earlier, who tried to introduce new product into the market, the manufacturer was held responsible for all of the company's errors. Incensed by this, the manufacturer retracted all of its discounting. It had taken a colossal risk by breaking off existing relationships with other dealers in the state, gambling everything on Bruce and Ted, who boasted success was inevitable.

Moreover, the manufacturer had gone above and beyond to ensure success. So, in addition to outstanding discounting, it had also offered factory training, engineering expertise, and put its entire customer service at the company's disposal. Even the territory rep for the manufacturer visited the company nearly every two weeks to answer any questions that may have arisen. And for all that the manufacturer did, Bruce tried to back-charge them thousands of dollars.

"You tell them that if they want to be in this market then they better start working with us," he said to the saleswoman, who was suddenly put in the middle. "After all, I'm not a bank." Bruce may have believed in building relationships, but his methods were entirely counterproductive. After that fiasco, the relationship was irrevocably tarnished. Threats were exchanged, and neither side was willing to put it behind them; the real victims however were the clients, who suffered overdue deadlines and excuses.

V.   <u>Accountability</u>

After a few weeks, Arthur was shaken. He had witnessed Bruce's stringency on others, but now experienced it for the first time himself. Tasked with cleaning up the mess left behind by a former employee, the one he had replaced, he discovered just how much fault lay with management as opposed to the person they wished to blame. Neither Bruce nor Ted would accept responsibility for their mismanagement nor were either willing to grant him any room to breath; they expected results overnight. Apparently, both were blind to the reality of the situation.

"My expectations are through the roof," Bruce said, upset with him. He neither wanted to hear the facts nor get excuses. "Buddy, this needs to be wrapped up without error." But repairing damaged relationships neither happened overnight nor were expected losses reversed without some sort of strategy.

As a fish rots from the head, Bruce first scorned him, and then Ted did. They accused him of negligence and threatened to fire him. "It's real simple buddy boy," said Ted, mimicking Bruce, "all you got to do is your job, and you'll be here forever. You'll never have to find another job."

And yet, the two were old dogs that refused to learn new tricks. For instance, Bruce interacted with clients the way he always had done: by pretending they had a closer relationship than what actually existed. He often sent informal emails to clients, as though the two were having a conversation in public.

"What's the word, buddy?" read one of his emails, asking whether the client was ready to sign yet. In another instance, his proposals were inaccurately written, leaving the company not just open to liability but also revealed to the client his lack of product knowledge; since Ted mirrored his proposals as well as speech, he too was at fault. Every proposal the two of them did was convoluted with useless factory jargon that was neither explainable to the client nor relevant to make the sale. In almost ever instance the client was confused on what he or she was getting as well as the price.

"Buddy, I know my market," Bruce said. "I've been doing this for thirty years." And yet, his closing rate was only good because of how exceptionally low he went on his margins.

Moreover, the team had little good to say about his management skills. By and large, most agents agreed that the sales meeting could be shorted if he just let them input their data into the spreadsheet. "He can barely type anyway," one agent said. "That's just another reason why we keep it so short. Otherwise, we'll be there all day!"

In listening to the team, micromanagement as well as negligence were the two largest grievances. "We don't even discuss goals or strategies," said another agent to Arthur. Most felt the sales meetings were highly unproductive.

"He doesn't even compromise," said another, noting his overbearing mechanisms. Bruce was simply too preferential in his ways to change or consider other's suggestions.

VI.   <u>Many Boasts</u>

But as inflexible as Bruce was Ted was the opposite, only he was so flexible that he was distant. As the Vice President of Sales, Ted was surprisingly aloof from both the concept of generating revenue as he was about saving the company money.

He frequently boasted about the business he once owned. "I ran it for years," he liked to say. "I had top accounts across the nation. I had a strong sales force, and then I lost it all." For whatever reason he always added that last part, inexplicably taking pride in his failure, as though it were a prerequisite to being a corporate executive.

But then again, Ted was a conundrum. His bonus was based on sales, but he rarely lifted a finger. Instead, he tried to get others to sell for him; in the course of ten months, he only ever pursued two leads, the same two in fact, and then lost one of them worth $750,000. He had come into the company with a string of high-end clients, but had neither expanded his clientele since then nor kept his expenditures down when entertaining existing clients: he once treated a client to a week of lunches, dinners and a ballgame, and yet gained nothing from it. In another instance, he spent over $1,000 entertaining a house client, only to then yield a $3,000 deal at 10% margin.

Moreover, he was rarely at the office. If his sales numbers were high then it might explain his absence, but every week he reported zero sales. Nevertheless, Bruce neither reprimanded him for that nor questioned his exorbitant spending. And even when he was at the office he went unnoticed, and so the team nicknamed Ted, "the ninja." Despite the fact that his office was at the end of the hall, few if any saw him pass by. Moreover, he did as little work as possible. Often, he just sent an email, and then called it a day. In one instance, it took him half an hour to send a one-sentence email.

VII. The Jock of the Office

If the weather was nice, Ted didn't bother coming into the office. Instead, he went golfing. On rare occasion he took clients with him.

* * * * * * * *

Now in his late fifties, Ted had neither any reservation to his opinion or any sense of censorship. He proudly boasted his hardcore sexual fetishes, often disclosing the fact that he slept with prostitutes regularly when he went abroad on sales trips.

"I roughed her up badly," he once said to a group of female co-workers, one of whom was the human resources director. Athletically built, he was also referred to as the, "Jock of the office," because every day he routinely ate his oatmeal bar for breakfast, two sandwiches for lunch, and a high protein meal for dinner, and every conversation was either about sports or exercise. Moreover, he always spoke in a way that demeaned other's lifestyles, as though his was better.

In addition, he always spoke to agents using sports metaphors, which were often lost or diluted by his habit of mixing sports together. "You can either punt it or rush it," he once said to a saleswoman. "But I want a hole-in-one." Perhaps it might have made sense if it had been about closing a deal. Unfortunately, it was said in regards to ordering from the factory.

In another case he used a baseball analogy. "There's three men on base and you're up to bat." Again, if he was trying to imply the pressure was on to close the sale then it may have made sense, but it wasn't. It was about wearing a different tie to work.

Each of his proved remarkably difficult to discern and too often resulted in substantial losses. In one case, an agent lost a deal worth $150,000 to which Ted angrily replied, "I hired you to do a job right." He then fired him.

Even Arthur couldn't escape the metaphors. Whenever he tried to talk business, the vice president simply replied in riddles. "I want that first-down," he said.

But even with Arthur's sports knowledge he could never construe the man's meaning. How was a first-down related to making a call to a vender? Not surprisingly, there was confusion, and more than once Arthur was pulled into the conference room, scorned by both Ted and Bruce.

"Buddy boy, what are you doing?" the vice-president said, incensed by Arthur's apparent failure for what seemed a simple analogy instruction. "I told you exactly what to do, and you did the opposite. Now this is the third down, and I don't want a fourth. I want a touchdown!"

But as negligent as Ted was in management and booking sales, he was even worse when it came to interacting with clients. His negotiation skills were almost nonexistent; whenever his quotes were questioned he went right to the price, offering to lower it if that would please the client.

This surprised Arthur, who for only being in the industry a few years could command any price he wished because he had learned how to negotiate. Price was the last thing he went to. In fact, Arthur had learned to avoid the questioning altogether by simply selling himself. If the client liked him then the price was worth it; his greatest profit margin ever had been 78% on a $48,000 deal ($37,440 profit).

In another instance, he and Arthur visited an existing client who was on the fence. A little salesmanship was all that was required, but instead Ted told Arthur to wait outside so that "the men could talk." Not surprisingly, the client was taken aback and subsequently ended the meeting.

It was then that Arthur began to re-evaluate his predecessor and the rumors that abounded about him, alleging that he was as disorganized as he had been a poor salesman. As Arthur discovered, neither were in fact true. His predecessor had in fact sold high and tried to stay organized, but it was the negligence of others that had sabotaged his efforts:

Whenever a problem or question arose, neither Ted nor Bruce was around. Thus, the man had to often make executive decisions that he was ultimately blamed for; in one instance, he apparently had tried to inquire about a detail, but owing to the absence of his superiors, he made a decision that cost the project its profit. Fortunately, the client agreed in writing to cover the difference, and yet when Arthur took over the project several months later he learned that Bruce had gone with the original price, so as not to "upset" the client.

Perhaps most disturbing of all about his predecessor's unfortunate dismissal was that Bruce and Ted gloated about it. They often shared it with venders and clients, taking pride where modesty or restraint should have been an order. As a result, and not surprisingly, venders and clients alike felt unsettled by it. Arthur couldn't understand it. Didn't they realize how belittling their former employee sounded to others? Were they not aware of how it reflected on them as managers? Apparently not because Ted especially loved to rant about it, and often would tangent just to speak of it. Not surprisingly, it discredited the company as a whole, and consequently cost it revenue.

VIII.   <u>Narrow-minded</u>

An agent once lost a $225,000 deal because of a
misinterpreted golf metaphor. In addition to blaming the agent
Ted made no attempt whatsoever to salvage the deal. Instead, he
simply told the client, "I understand. Have a nice day."

* * * * * * * *

Despite his stringent ways, Bruce had grown the company
with volume. And yet, as so many agents believed, the company
could have done so much better. "Don't bother getting me
$1,000," Bruce often said. "Just get me a $1." Despite an amazing
team of sales agents, he repeatedly tugged on the leash,
prohibiting them from making the company profit.

He even had access to a large talent-pool of human
capital, but he neither exploited its potential nor saw it as a
resource. In one instance after booking a major deal, he hired
twenty new staff employees to work a newly renovated part of

the office. Unfortunately, the contract expired after only a year and he subsequently dismissed them all; he neither gave any thought to tapping into that existing pool for positions elsewhere in the company nor trying to secure the contract for another year.

"Remember, he only thinks in one direction," said an agent to Arthur, who was taken aback by the large-scale dismissals. Arthur was dumbfounded why Bruce had not tried to secure the contract again. "That's the way the man is."

Arthur couldn't believe it. With all that manpower and talent in his lap, and Bruce just let them go. It was asinine. After all, he had once been on that side of the fence and was appreciative of being tapped by a manager: he had worked the 3 AM shift, sweating to earn his minimum wage. Hired in as one of ten seasonal helpers, his shift lead recommended him to the store manager, who let the rest go.

But with Bruce things were different. Everything operated without variation. He had no more qualms about letting talent escape than he did about dismissing agents who sold at high margins. Everything was ironclad. If he won the contract at a later date, then he would just hire new people. As one agent succinctly put it, "When $2 + 2 = 5$, then the man will open his eyes. Until then, the sky is falling."

The Numbers

IX.   Entertaining Clients

Narrow-minded, stringent, and refusing to be held accountable, Bruce suffered a $9,000,000 loss one year, and subsequently blamed it on an intern.

* * * * * * * *

Both Bruce and Ted spent enormous sums entertaining clients to win new business. The latter went after his existing clientele while the former targeted new clients. From frequently spending $500 on lunches to taking clients to the company stadium suite, the two secured few if any outstanding deals. In one instance, Bruce secured a deal worth $300,000, which at first seemed sizable, except that his net margin was so low that it hardly paid for the time spent trying to book it.

Refusing to learn new tricks, Bruce like Ted believed they knew exactly how to win business. "Money spent is money earned," the latter once said to Arthur. "That's the way it is, buddy." And between the two, the president and vice-president easily spent over $10,000 a month entertaining clients. And yet, their world suddenly came crashing down when Arthur began booking deals without spending a dime. At once they pulled him into the conference room to reprimand him.

"Buddy, what are you doing?" Bruce said, demanding an explanation. As much as he was intrigued to find out what his sales manager was doing, he was more livid at Arthur's deviation from the set way of doing things.

Ted too was incensed, but largely because his lifestyle was based around wining, dining and golfing. He was not about to let anyone unearth a secret that would turn his world upside down. "I don't know what you're doing, but this is not how you earn business," he said, scornfully.

"Buddy, I got to tell you," Bruce said, chiming in. "I'm not liking this. I'm hearing things that doesn't match how we do things here." Arthur was shocked. How was it possible he was being scolded for saving the company money? He didn't understand.

"You bid low, buddy boy," Ted said. "That's what we expect of you. You bid low, get the deal, and then build up the relationships. And I expect you to be buying bagels or taking clients out to lunch. From now on, I want to see more receipts from you!" Arthur was astonished. Taken aback, he was speechless. All he had done was use a simple salesmanship trick that he had learned in LA. It worked there, so he figured it would work here.

"Now I want to know how you're doing this," Bruce said, slapping the table. He was still agitated that Arthur had defied his time-honored dogma. The young man took a deep breath and told them that he just gave clients his card.

X. The Magic Card Trick

"I just give them my card," he said, but neither of them was in the mood for games. "Buddy, I don't have time for jokes, so you better start explaining yourself, and fast," said Bruce. "Everybody has business cards!" So, how was Arthur's any different? The young man pulled it out of his wallet and handed it to him. "It's blank," Bruce said, about ready to throw him out.

"Turn it over," Arthur said, despairingly. This wasn't how he delivered his card trick, but then he had never met anybody so opposed to saving money; it was a card trick that cost him almost nothing to make, and yet earned him hundreds of thousands of dollars in business, including a past five million dollar deal.

As Bruce turned the card over, he just stared at it. All at once, anger swelled in his cheeks and he crumbled it up and threw it at him. "This is the most absurd thing I've ever seen in my entire life!"

Simple, inexpensive and deliberately stupid, it worked like a charm every time, guaranteed. It had never once failed Arthur, and he booked more business with it than he had ever imagined possible. After all, it was all about humor. It gave his potential client a good laugh; it stopped people and gave them a reprieve from whatever was happening in their day. Even those experiencing a stressful day paused to chuckle.

My Card

But the card was useless without its delivery. Any salesman could whip the card out his pocket, but without a rehearsed script it was just like any other gimmick. And Arthur had practiced his delivery like a comedian telling a joke. He always read his audience first and foremost, judging both the reaction as well as timing.

He also learned ways to increase his chances by further preempting his potential clients with a light joke ahead of time. This helped ease the card in as well as gauge the client's sense of humor. In one instance, he presented it to a client who was developing several properties. The man chuckled, called him a smart aleck, and gave him all three properties.

But perhaps even more important than reading his audience was the secret in timing. Patience was everything. It was about waiting for that split-second when the client was ready for it, or better put, was unprepared to laugh; it was timing that helped booked a nationwide retail chain. His card wasn't magical, but the result of rehearsals. He had booked more business and saved more money than he ever could by entertaining clients; wasn't that the goal anyway? After all, the card also helped clients remember him, and that gave him a significant edge against his competition.

XI.   How to Earn Real Business

Ted once remarked how Arthur reminded him of himself at his age. Arthur begged to disagree. Nothing about the man ever helped anybody else.

* * * * * * * *

"Buddy, I have zero tolerance for liars," Bruce said, irate beyond belief. He had just crumbled the card up. "I see this as lying and being incredibly deceitful!" He was fuming. "Now I'm paying you a lot of money, so start doing what I tell you and take clients out!"

As Arthur was excused from the room, Bruce turned to his vice president. "I don't care what you have to do, but it's your bonus on the line, so get him straightened out!" Ted hated being reprimanded, or being held accountable, and made it very clear to Arthur after the meeting.

"From this point forward," he told him, furiously. "I expect to see more receipts out of you. I want you to start taking bagels to our existing customers, and I expect you to start taking clients out to lunch, or to our stadium suite. Is that understood?"

He even demanded to see Arthur's estimates, insisting that he review them before clients received them. "You're not bidding anything until I review it first, and enough of this high margin nonsense… you're not going to get the deals! And that goes double for that card. I never want to hear about that again!"

He was so indignant and annoyed that he took him to a lunch meeting just to prove his point. "I'm going to show you how real business is done." He invited a top-end client out to lunch and spent over $600. "Now that's how you do it," he said afterwards, securing a $100,000 deal at ten percent margin. Yet that same week, Arthur booked a contract using his card trick. It was worth $194,000 and he sold it at 36% margin ($69,840).

XII.   <u>Various Methods</u>

Bruce threw into a rage. "Buddy, how many times do I have to tell you, 10%! 10%! 10%! Nobody is going to give you work for more than that!"

* * * * * * * *

Arthur's card trick was virtually a guarantee for booking deals. It cost next to nothing to produce and if delivered properly it was a sure win. And yet, neither Bruce nor Ted embraced it. "There's no such thing as a guarantee," they said. But the proof was in the pudding, and as Arthur continued to bring in deals one after the next at high margins, the other two treated clients to lunch and to the company stadium suite with mixed results.

In once instance, Bruce took a prospective client to the suite and during the course of a conversation learned that the client's kid liked a certain player on the team. Abruptly excusing himself, Bruce went off to buy the jersey with the player's name on it. The client was taken aback and insisted on paying for it, but Bruce just asked him to repay the favor later on. "Just keep us in mind," he said. Unfortunately, when that time came the client looked the other way. It was a $600,000 lost bid.

Unfortunately, the more Arthur booked the more it incensed the other two. Whereas one felt his sales equation was being shattered the other felt his comfortable lifestyle was in jeopardy, but Arthur was just doing what he had been trained to do. In LA, he had been taught to sell as high as he could, if he could. Why spend the money if you can do it for nothing? As his mentor had instructed him before, a man named Victor, what mattered was closing the deal. Just how he did that was what separated him from his competition.

"Everybody has money in his or her pocket," Victor had told him. "All you have to do is figure out how to get it out." He had taught him to use humor as a way to lower the drawbridge. "Remember, people enjoy laughing. So make them smile." The man had pushed him to succeed. "Sell as high as you can. If you can get 100% profit margin, then do it."

Victor had embraced him like a son, and perhaps even more so than his own, which perhaps may have led to Arthur's termination in LA. Nevertheless, Arthur respected Victor for what the man had taught him; he had raised the bar repeatedly and Arthur never failed to disappoint him. "I want you to be better than me," the man had said, "and you will be!" Victor had been a positive influence in Arthur's life despite the negative events that had unfolded, and out of the man's teachings Arthur had booked his largest deal ever, five million dollars.

And yet, perhaps even more revealing between Victor and Bruce was the preferential treatment the former received. Whereas Bruce received last look, Victor was simply handed the work. His clients trusted him and could rely upon his talents; Victor priced high, but he knew his product and his reputation in the market sold himself. Whereas Bruce's clients shopped around, Victor's never did.

XIII. Earning Respect

Bruce wasn't so much against profit as he was against deviation. "The only way you're ever going to earn respect and business is by bidding low," he scorned Arthur, rejecting the young man's sales approach. Even with proof in the pudding he was reprimanded. "Bid low, buddy. That's what I keep telling you. When you bid low I promise you that you will get more work." And yet, in less than a year, Arthur earned substantially more from his card trick than by using Bruce's method.

Not only did he earn respect from his co-workers, but also his clients. In one instance, a client-CEO called upon Arthur instead of Bruce. The President responded by telling Arthur that he had no business communicating with him. "You're just a sales manager, buddy. That's not your place to be talking with him." But the client didn't see it that way.

XIV.   <u>High Margins</u>

During his ten-month employment, Arthur made several overtures to go with Ted on sales calls, but the vice president refused every time. "I don't have time to babysit you," he said. Unfortunately, the one time he finally did concede it cost Arthur a $56,000 deal, which had a potential profit of $35,000. As soon as they had arrived at the client's office the first thing Ted did was open his mouth, "So, how does it compare to others?" The client had been completely sold on Arthur and hadn't even considered shopping around.

* * * * * * * * *

After ten months, Arthur was unexpectedly called into the conference room. He expected another round of scolding, but instead was fired. "Can I ask why?" he asked, somewhat dumbfounded. He knew his sales approach had created some tension, but he doubted that was the reason.

Across from him sat Ted, who was straddled by either side by the human resources director and Sheryl, the Director of Operations. The former seemed uneasy, almost relunctant to be there. The latter just sat quietly, saying nothing.

"You're not meeting your quota," Ted replied.

Arthur looked surprised. "Can I ask what that is?" For ten months he had tried to get a number out of Ted.

"$350,000 in annual profit." Arthur shot a look of surprise. It wasn't that the number was high. On the contrary, he was amazed at how low it was! For certain he had already met it.

Aside from having almost no time to earn new business, he had nevertheless done so: in a period of ten months, he had cleaned up a hornet's nest of problems, including inaccurate estimates, wrong product ordered or sold, and a string of unhappy customers. It had been a problem that neither Bruce nor Ted nor even Sheryl had wanted to sort out, and so they had given it to, or rather dumped it on Arthur.

And Arthur certainly believed he had done a good job, correcting the mistakes, turning red into green and pleasing

41

disgruntled clients. He had given his word and delivered upon it, turning several dissatisfied clients into repeat customers; he managed the disaster-projects, earning the company profit and had the proof to show for it. In one instance, a project worth $65,000 had been expected to lose ten thousand dollars. Instead, he turned it around and made the company over $30,000.

In another instance, a project over two years old was now costing the company more than its initial contract. Expected to lose over $15,000, Arthur project managed it effectively and reversed its expected loses, earning the company only a $100, but certainly better than what everyone had expected.

He negotiated where he had to. He meticulously kept track of his paperwork, and maintained a constant flow of communication between the client and himself as well as his technicians. In total, he reversed nearly $300,000 in forecasted losses. But even more than that, he was certain he had met Ted's quota of $350,000 in annual profit: from new business, he had earned $26,000 in profit on a $40,000 deal, a 65% return.

And his high margins were a constant. In another, he earned $18,240 on a $48,000 contract, a 38% margin. In one month he booked just over $75,000 at a margin of 82%, earning the company roughly $62,000. Another time, he earned $15,000 on a project worth slightly over $25,000, an almost 60% return.

And in addition to new business and project managing, Arthur also booked several new service accounts at 50% margin. In his last month, Arthur booked just over $394,000 in profit, bringing his final total to over $630,000 in profit. It hadn't even been a year.

XV.   <u>Delegating Tasks</u>

Of the $630,000 in profit that Arthur earned for the company, most of it was earned largely by his card trick, his rigorous filtering process of sales leads, and his strategic planning with select manufacturers to leverage certain products in the market. Yet, despite every attempt to share his strategy, Ted never once wanted to listen to him.

* * * * * * * *

Yet, how did Ted not know about Arthur's success? After all, didn't he attend the sales meetings or put together the sales reports? The answers to those questions were, respectfully, on occasion and never. Ted often missed sales meetings, either sleeping in or finding some other excuse. When he did happen to attend his focus was less on sales and more on asserting his dominate role as second to Bruce.

And as far as the reports went, Sheryl did them, but as Director of Operations she neither had the sales information to properly fill out the spreadsheet nor even the wherewithal to ask for help. As a result, her reports were consistently erroneous; and with such improperly prepared documents submitted to Bruce every month it painted such a disfigured portrait of the company's current standing that Bruce often made ill-advised decisions.

But couldn't Sheryl have asked? Of course, but then, she already had too much on her plate as it was. Supervising almost a hundred employees she simply couldn't keep up, and the report was honestly the last thing on her list to do; too often she prepared it the night before it was due. Finally, overwhelmed, she capitulated to the stress and had a small nervous breakdown. From then on, she dressed over the top everyday, regressing into the saleswoman that she used to be when times were simpler; she donned high heels and an excessive amount of jewelry.

Being in operations was simply not her forte. It required a certain acumen that she neither possessed nor sought to achieve.

As a result, her solution to everything became pointing her finger and delegating. Unfortunately, she neither took accountability nor delegated tasks to the appropriate individuals. In one instance, she tasked a customer service problem to someone in accounting.

She delegated everything, relieving her of as much burden as she could. She set impractical deadlines, not because she thought they could or should meet them, but because it gave her an excuse when it came to hold someone accountable. In one instance, she insisted on a twenty-four time frame that in reality required a week. She frequently overburdened the Finance Department, often delegating minuscule tasks that were neither relevant nor important; in addition to being a distraction, it also inflicted undue stress, which the department neither needed nor wanted, especially with Bruce in a panic over the sales reports.

Moreover, she often tasked sales agents. In one instance, she gave a sales agent a list of existing clients and expected him to call on them. Unfortunately, the list neither contained names nor phone numbers. It just had the client's company names.

XVI.   Inaccurate Projections

Perhaps the greatest mystery of all in the office was why Sheryl was doing the sales reports to begin with. After all, she wasn't the vice president of sales. Ted was. Some figured it had to do with the fact that the ninja was never around, but some alleged that it was because Ted shied away from responsibility. Whatever the reason, the reports were always wrong.

Every month was the same. Bruce received them at the last minute and panicked. It was almost clockwork. To make matters worse, Sheryl didn't even understand the company software, which was needed to fill out the spreadsheet. Fortunately for her, Arthur did, and also fortunate for her that his office sat across the hall from hers.

"What were your numbers last month?" she asked, not even having the most basic information. Whereas one might view the sales meeting as a snapshot of how the company was in a particular week the sales reports was a more refined microscope... except that   nothing ever matched.

Too often, Sheryl made simple mistakes and rarely if ever corrected them when they were discovered, which often led to Bruce's cataclysmic panic. In one instance, an agent's actual costs for a project outweighed his estimated costs… and yet Sheryl goofed up and the company awarded him a bonus. In another instance, the saleswoman mentioned earlier who had earned 10% of her $450,000 bookings, or $45,000, had in fact lost all of it to her poor project management skills. Meanwhile, Arthur with $630,000 in profit had just $35,000, according to Sheryl's report; and to add icing to the cake, despite having a panic every month, Bruce neither questioned Sheryl's reports nor insisted that Ted check them over for accuracy.

To make matters even worse, whenever Sheryl asked for Arthur's help she often forgot to save it or simply saved it as something else, which she then later forgot what she had called it or where she saved it, thus resulting in her submitting to Bruce an older, inaccurate version.

XVII. <u>The Queen of Operations</u>

When Ted told Arthur he was terminated, he referenced Sheryl's report. Once again, it had been submitted inaccurately.

* * * * * * * *

In addition to being inaccurate, the sales report was almost always late. "You know how this works," Bruce said to her, scorning her for being tardy yet once again. "I need it every first week of the month."

"I just need another hour," she said, but whether she had another hour or another day it didn't matter.

"Buddy," he said impatiently. "I needed it yesterday! I already gave you another day. So, let's go already. I need it!"

Yet this was commonplace, and often because she portioned it out, delegating it people who had neither the information nor any idea of where to begin. Too often, she delegated it to the Finance Department, who threw it back at her.

Yet, by delegating it to others, she could then blame it on somebody else, which made her increasingly unpopular and steadily plunged company morale. It also earned her the infamous nickname as the "Queen of Operations," which many added the word "evil" in front.

XVIII.   A Sharp Drop off a Cliff

Most employees if not all resented Sheryl. As the fish rots from the head, she took no accountability for her mistakes. The more she pointed her finger the faster morale dropped, as did productivity. Only interns remained naively optimistic, that was until she put one in charge of the sales report. Few if any interns wanted to be blamed for a nine million dollar loss!

Overwhelmed and suffering a nervous breakdown, she could neither ask for help nor was anyone willing to give it, and she had a better chance of rock-climbing without support cables than asking for Ted's help. The vice president was either never around nor were his organizational skills any better. In fact, the Information Technology Manager once tried to find a file on his computer, but it was so jumbled that she gave up. Apparently, Ted had no idea how to even create some as simple as a folder on his desktop.

And so, Sheryl was on her own, submitting whatever she could, whether it was accurate or not. And not surprising, Bruce reacted in kind, often jumping ship as if the company were going under. In one instance, he suspended all hiring.

"I'm not a bank," he told his superintendent, Jimmy, who was inadvertently put into the difficult position of completing multiple projects with limited manpower.

"What do expect me to do?" he asked, frustrated. "I'm not a miracle worker!" Jimmy had known Bruce for over thirty years, and being so close to retirement, he didn't care what came out of his mouth. "You've got to give me more men, or you can just kiss all that money good-bye!"

Bruce shrugged his shoulders. "I don't know what to tell you. You got to do without, buddy." He knew Jimmy was resourceful, but what he didn't know was that Jimmy's foremen would start "robbing" from each other. Before anyone could stop them, foremen started grabbing laborers left and right to finish the work; right away, some projects went on hold.

"I need more men," Jimmy pleaded.

But Bruce just held up Sheryl's report. "I got no money coming in," he said. "What do you want me to do?" Instead of retirement, Jimmy was now scrambling. As deadlines were missed, customers began complaining and everyone started pointing the finger at him, including Sheryl.

Building Rapport

XIX. Processes, People and Profits

With missed deadlines, upset clients and Jimmy doing everything in his power to keep productivity from languishing, Ted demanded an explanation from his sales agents.

"When I receive a phone call from your client that means you're doing something wrong," he said, pulling them all into the conference room. "I should never receive any phone calls from your clients, period." But nobody had an answer. Every agent had done his or her job right. They had sold contracts, but now everything was going to hell. How was any of this their fault?

"I hired you to do a job right," Ted said, dismissing all of their complaints. "Now get this fixed." Then he left to go golfing.

In the meanwhile, as the superintendent tried desperately to contain the situation, the Finance Department came under heavy pressure to resolve the situation. Once again, Sheryl just pointed her finger. But Florence would not let that stand. Already exasperated with Ted's lack of turning in receipts, she was not about to take the blame for   another's misgivings.

A staunch woman, Florence had been with the company for over twenty years and was one of the few people who knew exactly how the software worked. A tenacious woman, she directed millions of dollars and knew exactly where every penny was; she demanded much from her team, but repaid it with respect and admiration. In one instance, she got into a heated argument. The employee insisted he had taken the afternoon off, scheduling that a month earlier, but Florence refused. As it started to escalate however, she drew a sigh and withdrew; she admitted that she knew he was right, but that she was overwhelmed and could really use his help.

"I'm sorry. I'm just under an incredible amount of stress," she said, exposing her vulnerability. The argument quickly subsided and the man agreed to stay an extra hour.

Although Bruce was the president, Florence ran the Finance Department and neither he nor the Almighty was going to dictate how she ran it; even when she had outpatient surgery she came into work to ensure questions were answered.

She always put her team first, serving as the vanguard against Sheryl, Ted and even Bruce. Too often it seemed everyone was willing to point the finger at her department, and she would not have it. When Bruce once called her up to ask her to move monies around she kindly declined until checking into it.

As a family person, her roots were well grounded in loyalty and support. She saw her team as one unit, and every year she allocated funds to an annual thank you party. Although it was never extravagant, it certainly accomplished what it was intended to do, implant a sense of pride and appreciation.

Her team respected her, and with her open-door policy she invited anyone in who had a question, even Jimmy, who often had a dirty joke to share. One time, the two of them were laughing when Arthur popped in.

"Why are you so different," Jimmy said, turning to him. "Nobody asks as many questions as you."

"Is that a bad thing?"

"Hell no, I wish more people did it," he chuckled.

"Really, nobody does, not even talk?"

"Nope. Here we're all just a bunch of islands… expect mine has babes in bikinis on it"

"No it doesn't," Florence said, knowing better.

"Yeah, I know. We're all just a bunch of fat guys, but hey, a man can dream can't he?"

XX. <u>Strengths and Weaknesses</u>

On several occasions, Arthur tried to build rapport with Bruce, but the engineer had no interest whatsoever. He neither inquired after his sales manager's progress nor shared a joke.

"Thirty years ago, I was just a lowly estimator on the ladder," he once told him. "Then one day, my boss had me come into his office and he said to me, 'Bruce why *did* you make a profit on this project?' Well I didn't know," he said, throwing his hands up. "I just figured my boss would've been happy that I did, because up until that point I was just getting work. So, I told him that and you know what he did?" Arthur shook his head. "Well, I'll tell you what he did. He threatened to fire me! And that's when it hit me," he said. "It's not about how much money you make. It's knowing how you made it."

Ever since then Bruce was dogmatic. He knew he could make money at 10% profit margin, and so he insisted that nobody went higher.

He once applauded an agent who earned 10% on a $400,000 sale, and yet reprimanded another agent who earned just two points higher. "Just get me a dollar!" He believed that ten percent profit margin was just enough of the market pie to grow a business and own a custom built home on waterfront property. In his mind, he envisaged his employees like an assembly line, arriving promptly at 8 AM, conducting business at 10% margin, and then leaving precisely at 5 PM.

"The only way a company succeeds is when everyone moves in the same direction and pace, like wheels on a car."

To Bruce, steady growth was conservative growth. He appreciated Arthur's eagerness to close deals at higher margins, but he refused them. "Forget about making me a thousand dollars. Just get me a dollar." To him, 10% margin was survival in good and bad times. And yet, he was a man who saw far, but had short arms. If he were trapped in the wilderness, Bruce would certainly pick berries, preferring smaller portions to stalking a large prey for days; he favored lesser but more reliable results than taking seemingly risky ventures.

Unfortunately, the thought of picking berries *and* hunting were neither put together. Sometimes a salesman had to go after small deals as well as large deals. But to his credit, the company had grown over the last decade despite the recession, just not as well as it could have. Although the company was in the process of acquiring other enterprises it was collapsing internally: despite his $2,200,000 deal, Bruce's profit only came from whatever profit he had on his labor numbers, which was barely 10%.

Whereas he was content with nuggets, Arthur went for bullion. Of Bruce's $2.2 million deal the company earned about $220,000. And yet, in LA, Arthur's $5 million deal earned 28% profit, or $1,400,000. Moreover, what Arthur did in his last month, $394,000, was what others did in a year.

XXI. Conversations

On his birthday, Bruce received a card signed by everyone in the office. Inside was a gift card to a spa. He kept the card but threw away the gift. "Why do I need it?" he asked. "I already have a hot tub."

* * * * * * * *

As narrow-minded as Bruce was, Ted was even worse. He neither understood the gravity of the mess Arthur had to clean up nor inquired after his progress. Instead, he either went golfing or dined at expensive restaurants with clients. He enjoyed his comfortable lifestyle and refused to be handed any stress.

"I hired you to do a job right," he frequently said, always putting the responsibility on others. Neither his sales team nor the company's laborers respected him; he rarely set foot on a project site, and even Jimmy had to agree with his foremen that

Ted was a buffoon. He didn't know a hammer from a screwdriver.

Moreover, Jimmy had taken a trip abroad with him to visit a manufacturer, and in addition to the vice president gloating about his sexual exploits he also bragged about how much he was going to sell of that manufacturer's product. Instead, he just talked about selling it for the rest of the year.

He neither wished to be informed of Jimmy's progress nor Arthur's. Instead, he looked forward to teeing off, and once noted on Arthur's performance review how he, "inappropriately used management's time." He was just trying again to ask the vice president when they could visit clients together. Ironically, Bruce gave Arthur a 4 out of 5 on his review.

XXII. <u>Priorities</u>

After several failed attempts at talking with Ted, Arthur asked another agent if she experienced the same. "He doesn't talk with you," she said, rather surprised. "He's always talking with me!" Arthur wondered why that was.

"That's Ted for you," she said, trying to excuse him.

"What do you mean?"

"You don't know?" she asked, even more surprised.

He had seen Ted with female agents before, but never connected the dots. Now the light bulb went off. Ted was sexist, or at least that's what the female sales agents believed; within their small circle his sexual harassment was common lore.

Ted did not accompany females because he liked their company. He did it because he had no confidence in them. "It's a tough market out there," he once said to a female agent, referring to her gender as "too tender."

In another instance, he encouraged an agent to boast her "female qualities," noting that more cleavage would be far more "professional."

Moreover, Ted often spoke of his mail-ordered-bride, using provocative remarks and noting how she "did as a good wife should." She prepared his oatmeal breakfast bar and lunch as well as cooked his dinner. He typified her as a child, meek and incapable without his virile prowess protecting her; he mentioned how he covered her from head to toe every night with his "manliness," and how she took it "like a good girl."

He indulged her ambitions, which he referred to as "adorable," such as her wanting to get a driver's license. "It's so cute," he said to the human resources director. And yet while being married, he boasted about his practice of "breaking the jetlag," which was him perusing the street corners for prostitutes, or as he put it, "selecting from the stock on the shelves." After having sex with one Chinese prostitute, he proudly said, "I drilled that hole to China."

XXIII. Maximizing Dollars

When Jimmy went with Ted abroad, the vice president returned to their hotel room at 4 AM to proudly announce his sexual triumph by flexing his muscles like a champion.

* * * * * * * *

Of all the projects Arthur had to clean up, only one went to Sheryl since it was expected to make a substantial amount of money, $60,000 in profit. And yet, somehow she went into the red by forty thousand dollars. When Bruce demanded an explanation, she simply blamed it on Arthur as well as others.

Another time, a sales agent gravely misquoted and now faced a potential loss of over $50,000. Arthur sprang into action and met with the client; within a half hour he had sold the client on an alternative product at a slightly reduced value: the agent now made $55,000 in profit.

In another instance, Arthur was in the midst of aiding a saleswoman when Ted abruptly interrupted; since this was one of his clients, he felt obliged to say something. Without thinking, he obnoxiously disparaged the female agent in front of the client, apologizing on behalf of her gender. "It is what it is, but else can you expect? The client was so appalled that he rescinded the contract. It had been worth $225,000.

XXIV. Teamwork

Even in winter, Bruce got his car washed daily. He once got into an argument with the car wash owner, who had to explain that his unlimited monthly pass did not interpret to mean four times a day.

* * * * * * * * *

Arthur enjoyed visiting Florence's office. In exchange for teaching him how to use the software, he supplied her with sales information. "It still amazes me that you want to come in here," she said, still in disbelief at his friendliness. "It's not in our culture to do that." For all of Ted's ranting about it being a great company, few if any communicated, fearing reprisal or liability; being friendly simply did not exist, largely owing to the fact that blame was always passed: since neither Ted nor Sheryl stepped up that meant anyone was a target for fault.

Moreover, the two religiously copied others on their emails in order to absolve their actions later on; it was not uncommon for them to throw others under the bus, Ted in particular was notorious for this. On more than one occasion, he copied the client when ridiculing Arthur, as though somehow believing public humiliation reflected well on him as his boss.

But Florence neither engaged in that behavior nor encouraged it. She considered it treachery and anti-culture. After all, how did throwing the blame around implant trust? "How can my department work better with yours should be the culture around here," she said to him. "But how do you do that when someone has a knife at your throat? They tell you to do your job right, but isn't communicating a part of that job?"

She had a point, but neither Ted nor Sheryl would listen. It was just easier to point the finger than it was to step up. "It's about owning your accountability. If you lead others, then you own every decision and be that leader." Her son was an army lieutenant.

"You think that's what happened to the guy before me?"

"Beyond a doubt," she said. "He had his flaws, just like any of us, but his biggest mistake was that he let them push him onto an island as far out to sea as possible. I mean, how do you tell somebody to do their job right and then take no responsibility supervising that individual?"

Arthur understood. He had seen that lack of ownership before back in college when he participated in the Reserved Officer Training Corps (ROTC). He enjoyed the program, but some of the cadets were severely wanting in accountability.

As a squad leader, he interacted with other squad leaders, drilling alongside them and learning from their mistakes; in most instances, their mistakes cost mock lives. One time, they were drilling at night and Arthur's unit was lost in the woods, but morale was high, despite exhaustion and dehydration. Crossing a needle thicket in pitch black as well as traversing ankle deep mud, they finally saw the barracks and picked up the pace. As they congratulated one another on making it another squad leader boasted that his unit had reached the barracks sooner.

"But you're missing two in your squad," Arthur said, pointing out the obvious fact.

"Like that matters. They're probably still lost out there."

Another time, his squad was moving through the woods when the field instructor unexpected shouted, "Sniper!" Everyone ran for cover, taking shelter behind trees.

"Does anyone see him?" he shouted over to Alpha team, but saw nothing, and neither did Bravo. "Ideas," he said, reaching for other's suggestions before resorting to an impulse decision; it was a drill he had had his unit rehearse. Arthur believed in sharing accountability, so whatever his squad came up with was their decision too; owning that decision inspired not just good ideas, but also resolve: everyone was committed once the decision was made. So as Alpha flanked, Bravo lay down suppressive fire in the direction that the alleged sniper was in. "Excellent work squad leader," the instructor said, complimenting his quick and decisive action.

"Thank you sir," Arthur said, "We all did a great job."

"This program is about leadership, squad leader."

"Yes sir, I know that sir, but I could not have succeeded without my unit, sir."

The instructor nodded, impressed. "Congratulations squad leader. That's the second lesson of the day, and you're the first one today to learn it."

Like Arthur, Florence valued her team and owned every decision she made; she neither passed blame nor retreated from accusations that were founded. She didn't care if somebody didn't like her decisions. She stuck by them. She was responsible for the company's money and even Bruce learned to respect her fortitude.

Camaraderie

XXV. <u>Dirty Jokes</u>

Of the hundred laborers, foremen, warehouse crews and office staff that Sheryl managed she knew few of their names. Too often, she just referred to them as "you," or "that guy over there."

* * * * * * * *

After college, Arthur had used what he had learned in ROTC in his sales. He collaborated with others to achieve success, building rapport among co-workers, and establishing trust to drive results. Subsequently, his style of culture tripled his last company's revenue in less than two years during an economic recession, and he had hoped to extend those results in Cleveland.

In just ten months he not only doubled his quota, but also restored company trust by improving camaraderie between employees and upper management. Yet, his untimely termination not only led to a spike in antipathy and mistrust, but also accelerated the company's   implosion.

Since Sheryl directed her orders through Jimmy, she neither saw any need to remember the names of those in her department nor any reason to point her finger at anyone else. In one instance, she fabricated a parts list for a client, passing it off as a legit list from the factory. The ruse was discovered however, and she quickly blamed it on him.

"How can it be my fault when I delegate tasks," she said lying to the incensed client. "I tell everyone that I need to check it first. Clearly this person did not do that."

Few if any respected Sheryl, especially after that fiasco. And once again, it proved why so many went to Jimmy to vent and escape the absurdities of upper management, who aside from being the company's professional problem solver was also the company's clown. He had a niche for making others laugh, and forgetting about the irrationalities they were faced with.

"I think I'd be great in customer service," he said, chuckling ahead of the punch line. "I'm the dirtiest old man alive." Crude and depraved, his jokes once made the human resources director blush.

"You gotta have fun," he said, snickering at his own potty mouth. "I'm air pollution. I ruin so many virgin ears with my filthy puns." Fond of being somewhat offensive, he excused any lewd joke with contagious laughter. "Life's all about having fun, brother," he said. He enjoyed making others smile just about as much as he enjoyed laughing himself; he often could be found with two or three employees in his office, even the human resources director.

"Come on girl, you know that's funny," he said, chuckling. His comedic relief was as dirty and raunchy as an outhouse, but it was always welcomed and treated as a reprieve from the insanity of the office.

XXVI. The PPS

As a professional problem solver, or PPS, Jimmy was as detailed as he was methodical. Assessing the big picture, he accounted for everything. When Bruce hired twenty new employees for his new service contract, he turned to Jimmy to remodel the office; if anybody could accomplish it in a short period of time at minimal cost it was Jimmy.

With over forty years in the industry, he had seen and heard it all. With his expertise, he trained his foremen well, expecting each one of them to perform without his supervision; far from micromanaging he believed a person could do a job right with the proper training and belief.

He entrusted his foremen to oversee projects worth millions of dollars, reminding each of them that he was just a phone call away if they ran into problems; he believed in his foremen and in return they respected him.

"It's all about giving respect," he said to Arthur, who often turned to him with questions. "When you give it, you get it back and that helps when trying to solve hard questions, and in this industry that's all we have."

Arthur found Jimmy's technical expertise invaluable in both bidding as well as assisting him project management. One day, he noted how often Arthur came to see him.

"You know how many times he has come to see me?" he asked, referring to the vice president.

"How many?"

"Zero. And guess how many projects I have had to clean up of his." Arthur shook his head. He had no idea.

"Every last one of them."

Arthur was shocked, but Jimmy was somebody who could do the impossible. He once salvaged an $800,000 dollar deal that had been erred by Ted. And yet, the vice president neither thanked him nor even took him out to lunch.

"I did my job right," Jimmy said, hating that line.

XXVII.   A Glass Wall

Jimmy was also easy to talk to and always made time for others "I'm always available, brother," he said. Approachable as he was friendly, he wasted no time vacationing people from their headaches. "We're all in this together," he said, understanding the anxiety that Ted, Sheryl and often Bruce put their staff under. "If I can't help you, then we're all screwed."

For Florence, he especially went out of his way to alleviate her stress, often popping in her doorway, whether to spring a joke or just say hi. "Girl, you're killing me. When are you going to take a lunch with the guys and me? We'd love your company."

She thanked him, but always declined. Officially, company credit cards could not be used for employee lunches, but the loophole was when employees went together, and Jimmy was all about loopholes. Grabbing as many as he could get, he was went with twelve guys.

"I eat, and so do you, so why don't we go out and eat together... oh wait, that sounded kinda dirty," he said with a quick snicker. Even Arthur tagged along a few times, capitalizing on the opportunity to build rapport with others; whereas Ted overlooked the value of respect, Arthur embraced it.

And as Arthur discovered, the warehouse crews that often joined Jimmy for lunch had much to say about Ted. Apparently, the man was neither well liked nor respected. "I mean, he's never once set foot in the warehouse," said one worker. "It's like he doesn't even know we exist!"

Jimmy quickly stepped in. "That's because you're doing your job right," he said, mocking Ted. Everyone laughed.

XXVIII.   <u>The Right Man for the Job</u>

Arthur nearly had a $2,000,000 deal closed when Ted unexpectedly offered the client 20% off. Instead of leaping at the discount, the client instead reacted with suspicion and postponed the project indefinitely; his relationship was with Arthur, not Ted.

* * * * * * * *

Conversing with Jimmy, his foremen as well as the warehouse crews helped Arthur tremendously in managing his projects. In one instance, he was certain his $125,000 project could not have succeeded without them. "That's what we're here for brother, and also the laughing and bad jokes."

In talking with them, Arthur learned that neither the concept of rapport nor respect was considered important by upper management; apparently, Ted had never once spoken to a warehouse crew. "Wait, what? He's never talked with you?" Arthur found that hard to believe. And yet, it was true.

Ted just expected everyone to do their job right, believing in the process, not the people. "What's the point of you giving me respect when you just expect me to do my job right," a crewman said, frustrated by maltreatment. "But you know what really eats me is that I don't even know what he does here."

Everyone nodded. "I mean, yeah sure, he's the vice president, but what does he do? I mean if he doesn't bring in sales then what else does he do?"

"Whatever he does, he does it right," Jimmy said, half-jokingly. He had to agree with his co-worker though. Ted had neither set foot in the warehouse nor even in his office. "You have to understand something about that man," the superintendent added, getting serious. "The way that man sees the world is a lot like putting something in the microwave. You just expect it to be warm when it's done."

Arthur was simply stunned. To him, it was a gross expectation to presume others should simply do their job right without any respect or acknowledgement given. And yet to Ted, that was exactly how an executive should operate. From start to finish, he believed there was no point in exercising interaction.

Moreover, doing one's job right meant making no mistakes, and so therefore it made no sense to him to recognize someone for doing a "good job," when they were just supposed to "do their job right" to begin with.

"Look, there's high expectations," said Jimmy, "and then there's just an excuse from being held accountable. And if I tell you to do your job right, and you go and make a mistake and somehow I'm free of any responsibility. Well then, frankly, that's bullshit, in my opinion. I say, own up, hold yourself accountable, and if you set high expectations, then I better see you setting the example."

XXIX. Shards of Glass

Jimmy told Arthur that six others had been sales manager before him. "And not one of them ever did what you're doing. I mean how hard is it to come over and talk with somebody, get to know them and build some respect?"

* * * * * * * *

With Bruce's stringent policies, Ted aloof, and Sheryl pointing her finger, the writing was on the wall. And as the company tiptoed on the threshold of collapse, the vice president continued to boast how much of a great place it was to work. "This is the last company you'll ever work for," he often said.

Yet, in just the last five years the company had higher turnover than it had ever experienced before; sales agents and laborers alike had either quit or were terminated.

Ted's infamous line not only deepened the wound of morale, but evoked cynicism of upper management as well as resentment; dovetailed with

Sheryl's finger-pointing and productivity declined even further; with erroneous reports and hiring freezes, the finger pointing only exacerbated.

Even training became almost nonexistent. Typically, Jimmy maintained a continuous program, but his focus had been distracted and now laborers were lacking basic course education or renewal certifications; onboard training for every new employee was even further reduced to watching an outdated safety tape that displayed current mandatory standards as simply "suggestions for good housekeeping."

Perhaps even more revealing was that the company core values were either skirted or ignored, including accountability and performance excellence; less noteworthy, but still peculiar was the fact that the other three core values were simply different variations of the same word. Honesty, Integrity, and Trust.

With increasingly high turnover, negligent management as well as restrictive policies, the morale of the company slipped.

XXX.   The Line is Drawn

The one time Arthur went with Ted, the vice president took out a small rug from his trunk to put under Arthur's feet. He didn't want any dirt on his car floor.

* * * * * * * *

As morale plunged, disgruntled employees infected others with their dissatisfaction, spreading disfavor throughout every department. Even Florence struggled to keep her team happy.

Disillusioned by Sheryl's reports, the Finance Department came under intense pressure from Bruce to remedy the situation; he obstinately refused to believe Sheryl had erred. "Buddy, you're in charge of the numbers," he said to Florence. "Get our house in order."

Within hiring suspended, disenchantment also spread even faster among the foremen, who found they were doing double the work for the same pay.

Despite several overtures, such as gift cards, Jimmy's foremen had had it. One walked right off the job, leaving a $4,500,000 project unfinished; neither his replacement nor the fellow hired even after him could pick up the pieces, and so Jimmy had to take it over. In another instance, a project manager became so overwhelmed by the compounding problems that he was hospitalized; when several employees inquired after his health, Ted simply remarked coldly that the man had brought it upon himself. "He didn't do his job right."

That display of insensitivity was the last straw. Now nothing could stem the erosion. Positions lay vacated, and morale plunged as more and more responsibilities were put onto others, and yet in the meanwhile, Ted went to the golf course.

Day by day, the situation exacerbated. And as it worsened, Sheryl began leaving the office earlier; in her absence, more and more people came to Arthur for assistance. He began coordinating logistics, overseeing the project management of others, improving the service side of the business by adding additional accounts and increasing prices, and also worked much more closely with Florence. By the time he was terminated, he was keeping multiple departments afloat while still cleaning up the mess and booking new contracts.

XXXI. Knowing the Market

In a final effort to build cohesion with Ted and Bruce, Arthur bid a five-year public contract. It was an ideal opportunity to add both service numbers as well as new product over the course of several years. Moreover, it would no doubt bolster the company's network of contacts in the public sector.

"We are solid," Ted told Bruce, having only glanced at Arthur's numbers briefly. "I'm confident of our success. There's not a chance that we can lose this." With Ted's approval and Bruce's subsequent signature, Arthur bid it. Unfortunately, the results were anything but expected. Instead of outdoing the competition, the carpet was pulled from under them: of a bid worth $425,000 the next bidder on the list was in the low $300,000 range. So, either the competition was giving it away, or neither Bruce nor Ted truly understood their market. To make matters worse, the bid had consumed nearly three weeks of Arthur's time. In the past, he would have filtered it to pursue other ventures, but he wanted to build rapport with them, and also Ted insisted had that he bid   it.

Implosion

XXXII.   Early Attempts

"Buddy, you got to know your costs!" Bruce snapped at him. Arthur had no rebuttal. He had just lost a five-year contract bid that Bruce had not only reviewed, but also signed. Meanwhile, Ted was out golfing.

* * * * * * * *

The five-year contract was the last major effort to build cohesion. Early on, Arthur had tried to collaborate with Bruce, hoping to understand how the man thought; perhaps if he knew how the man ticked then he might be more successful. After all, who apparently knew the market better than Bruce? Yet, in one instance, the two of them bid an $85,000 deal to a public utility. Throughout the process, Bruce bragged about his network connections, including the utility's purchasing agent. And yet, when they paid a visit to the agent the man was less than happy to see them.

"Don't you have anything better to do than to come and see me?" he asked. Apparently, Bruce's impressions of his connections were somewhat slanted. When they bid two more projects to the same agent, it came as no surprise that they lost them; four weeks later and $271,000 pursued in vain and the only thing Arthur had to show for it was Bruce's finger pointing.

Despite trying to collaborate, Bruce blamed the losses on him, alleging that he had never lost a bid to that particular agent in the past. So whatever went wrong was no doubt Arthur's fault; in addition to blaming him for inaccurate costing, he further reprimanded him for trying to follow up with the client, asserting that that was his responsibility.

"Buddy, let me follow up. He won't talk with you," he said. And yet, Bruce neither followed up with the man nor accepted ownership for failing to do so. "Buddy, you got to remind me. I do a lot of things every day."

XXXIII.   Alternatives

With the failure of the five-year contract, all hope was lost to build cohesion. Two weeks later, Arthur was terminated.

* * * * * * * * *

The president neither owned up to his misgivings nor considered the suggestions of others to improve the efficiency of the company. In the past, he had received proposals to improve the sales meetings, but when he dismissed every single one of them.

"Buddy, I've been doing this for a long time," he told a saleswoman, who subsequently quit afterwards. "I know what works and what doesn't." He rejected any substitutes in the way he managed or sold, or even to whom he sold to; Arthur wasn't the first one to note the purchasing agent didn't like Bruce.

But the perennial issue always remained the sales meeting. It was the bane of every sales agent, who viewed it not only as inefficient but also as a waste of money. Doing the math, the average agent was paid $42 an hour, and there were at least a dozen agents in the room. If Ted and Bruce were also counted then this equated to $504 an hour that the company spent on its employees; for a two hour minimum sales meeting this was $1,008 spent, which multiplied by 52 weeks equated to a final total of over $52,000 a year.

Moreover, since the meeting ran an average of two hours, this equated to 104 hours a year spent of agents sitting and waiting silently, mostly doing nothing but listening. Multiplied by at least a dozen people in the room and almost 1,250 hours were spent either fidgeting or helplessly watching the phone ring.

XXXIV.   A Round Robin

With sales and operations in disarray, the writing was on the wall. As laborers walked off the job, foremen either quit or were terminated for "poor job performance;" project managers were dismissed that failed to bring projects in on time and within budget. And the one person that needed to own up left early and pointed her finger.

With erroneous reports, hiring was sacrificed to the economy of the company, but as the numbers failed to match up even more strain was put on Florence's Department, who spent nearly half its time now vindicating itself from blame. And as sales agents resented the stringent policies, most either quit or simply learned to do what Sheryl and Ted did, point the finger.

XXXV. Iceberg

Despite everything he did, Jimmy lost control of his men.

Foremen he had known for years suddenly quit on him; Bruce

dismissed many of them and failed to tell Jimmy, leading to a

series of explosive arguments and setbacks in productivity.

To make matters worse, those he had known for years

accused him of being as negligent as Ted and Bruce; even

Florence experienced similar persecution from her staff. One

accountant got into a heated argument with her on a Friday

afternoon; the shouting escalated so loudly that even the

warehouse crews heard it. As Florence's department splintered,

Ted remarked that it was one again proof of why men should be

in charge of money.

XXXVI.   The Sinking of the Ship

And so as Ted teed off and Sheryl left as early as she could, the accruing resentment and agitation amongst employees reached a tipping point, finally boiling over with Arthur's dismissal.

In addition to increasing profit margins, lowering expenses, improving camaraderie as well as productivity and communication, he had also shouldered responsibilities of departments that were not his; he earned both the gratitude and admiration of others, and his untimely and unfortunate dismissal proved to be the beginning of the end. As he was escorted out, many more jumped ship. In his heart, Arthur knew he had done everything in his power to try and grow the company. But where one door closes another opens, and the following day his phone rang. It was another employer, eager to have him come aboard.

www.ingramcontent.com/pod-product-compliance
Lightning Source LLC
Chambersburg PA
CBHW060625210326
41520CB00010B/1473